Blue Prairie of Darkness

Jan Mordenski

Michigan Writers Cooperative Press
P. O. Box 2355
Traverse City, Michigan 49685

ISBN: 978-1-950744-30-5

Book design by Amy Hansen

Contents

BLUE PRAIRIE OF DARKNESS

Birds

I. Balanced on a wire in winter, they are the black beads of an abacus,
the cold black beads that shift the overdue accounts of the days.
Puffing up their feathers, they hold firm, worrying if the credit
of the airy years can cover their accumulating debt to the sky.

II. Spring writes its own list of chores—house cleaning, home building,
the nestful tending of eggs. But there's also the music—the circling
and bowing to each other in wild, unscripted dances, the folksongs
sung from branches, walls, from the dark thickets of memory.

III. Summer brings its long, silent hours of sun, its careful
hours of reflection, rest. Only in the arid dusk, the wavering dawn,
will there be the chance of sociability—meals, messages relayed
on the merest scraps of chatter, dreams of the yawning horizons.

IV. And in the fall labor recommences, the foraging, the battening of bodies
and spirits that any migration requires. Who's to say, when they pack
their little pin-feathered bags, what they choose to take with them—a twig
of nostalgia, a hard seed of longing, a compass, a flask of cold caution.

Whippets

Rather than of nature, you are more creatures of fantasy,
of dreams, what with your haughty snouts, dark wide eyes,
taut bodies tapering to hardly any body at all,
just enough muscle, enough hair, to connect four strong,
slim legs that will skim the muddy tracks at Dublin.

It figures that it was in Ireland I first saw you,
late in the bright summer evenings, after dinners, after
the cows had been marched home across the fields. I'd see
a wily fellow bobbing above the long stone fences, four
or five of you pulling him down the thin, wavering roads
of the strands, running your six prescribed miles, your
feet hardly touching the dark green land.

One lad said keeping you was like taking a wife, or
children, so extensive was the care you required.
And it is no wonder that Irish men have taken to you,
that they were the first ones to put a leash on
you furry long-shots, you thin, young living
chances that will one day, so hopefully, catch
the frail sail of the wind, and—suspended between
air and land, touching neither, pushing against both—
turn round the track and make of this gritty life a brief
but glittering victory, a round crowd of voices
cheering just you and no one else but the man who's,
so long, held the handle of the dream, running behind you.

The Poetry of Squirrels

is frenzied, frantic, its words as tight as kernelled
seeds, arranged in short lines of fricative consonants,
or spun loose in a musical mesh of open vowels.

It can be nattering, narrative, relaying the furzed sagas
of winters past, sheltering in place, leaving home,
roaming the fertile earth, climbing then nesting
in the strong arms of maples, sycamores, elms.

Often lyrical, nature-oriented, it can describe the sun
as it walks the worn wooden bridge of the sky,
or leaves as they dandle in the autumn's fired light,
the fancies of flight, the exhilarative peace of ascension.

Though careful and cadenced, it can also be mean,
its chittering sentences delineating, in scurried detail,
the common catastrophes of wind, snow, famine, disease,
the ever-present dangers of the paved road, unguarded field.

And the poetry is hungry, always hungry;
full of the rock-hard struggle for subsistence,
it whispers in the airy night, rants at the injustice
of industry, long hours, so little respect, so little pay.

Essentially, it is contradictory in nature—it chatters,
it whistles, it squeaks yet, so often, is silent, subversive,
surreptitious, as loud as the sunset, as quiet as the dawn.

It is cautious yet curious, free yet confined,
revelatory yet full of the hard-shelled mysteries
of life lived between the heavens and the earth.

Boisterous, rambling, it is passed among the members
of its closed society down the endless trunk of time;
precise, perfunctory, it sings nostalgically, triumphantly,
of the open path, the open sky, the occasional open palm.

China Dogs

December 1983 marked the ban on the ownership of dogs in Peking.
Over 200,000 dogs had been killed, many of them by their own
masters, in the six weeks previous to that ruling.
                                    The Detroit News, December 1983

In posses they searched you out
under the porches, between the charming
thickets of those sneaky gardens, up from back alleys,
the shops, the schoolyards, respected homes,
from the unsteady hands of the elders, sticky paws
of the children, the leashes, the chains and makeshift pens:
Peking would be dogless in December.

For six weeks a growling wailed the city,
wound its heart like a ticking toy,
chased itself like littered wind.

The government was in on it right from the start:
after examination it was apparent some sold the state meat.
Others thought clubbing the most merciful way;
cowards sought weighted bags from grass, from grain,
a little something in your food,
a slight maniacal snap of the leash.
It was better this way. Cleaner. Safer.
The people would chance to survive.

Today it is snowing a white and swirling snow.
Bones are cold. Eyes are narrowed to the wind.
The city heels in tense and tender silence.
Doors open freely. The moon hangs unaccompanied in the sky.
Somewhere in the mind remains the shadow of a wagging tail.

An Instrument of Peace

Years ago, in Galway, where a garden of foxglove
and rhododendron gave way to wilder things,
I leaned against a low stone wall to play
the tin whistle—*Gentle Maiden, Salley Gardens* . . . .

The afternoon was still enough, black bees
buzzing, salmon splashing the stream,
keeping time, and the air sweet with
summer grass and clover.

And so it was that a ring of heifers gathered silently
at my back, against my neck the gruff breath
of cows, coming, I don't know, out of respect
for the music, the mere curiosity of a girl

lost in the lure that is Ireland. And when I stopped,
just as quietly, they moved on, swaying, nodding.
Only then did I dare turn about. Recollection,
I can tell you, is an unselective gift.

Chiquita

The dog, she said, only spoke Spanish;
after all, she was *un perro callejero*, a street dog
brought up from Costa Rica when her daughter
returned from studying there. So I did my best
when I walked the scraggy little fluff, tried to remember
to look into her bright eyes when I spoke to her—
buen perro, vamos, deténgase—gently tugging at the leash
she regarded as absurd—as if she were going anywhere.

When we played games during those dog-sat days I learned
frisbee—*disco volador*, where's the ball—*donde esta
la pelota*. Mealtimes required a dictionary of translation:
chicken—*pollo*, carrots—*zanahorias*, potato chips—*papas fritas*.
But *no problema*—hunger, generally, translates into any language.

It was only years later, when Chiquita suffered a kidney infection,
that things got complicated. How do I say *No, you have to
take the pill. Peanut butter? How about cream cheese?
Take it; you'll feel better.* especially when I knew
that was not an accurate translation of events. How to say
*This cannot cure you, only numb you, make you sleep so,
for a while, you forget the pain.*

Worse yet, it was I who was to take her for her last visit
to the vet's. Her mistress wanted to be there
but it was a Tuesday, eight a.m., and there was work.
How, that cruel bright morning, to say,
*I don't know where you're going but it'll be a nice place.
There'll be grass, fields. You'll run again. You won't remember
hurting.* all the time wondering if there were words to say
*Where you're going, you won't likely remember me either.
El último viaje es silencioso.*

(Translation of proverb: *The final journey is a silent one.*)

                                    JAN MORDENSKI

Herd

On Stradbally Strand we sat, immobile,
in our Fiat, while Donal Mullligan
drove past us his cows, we three women,
eyes to eye with these heifers who looked
like beauty queen hopefuls—Daphne,
Gwendolyn, Marguerite—or like pastel
saints—Agatha, Anastasia, Claire—or like
women you'd see waiting outside the shops—
Dorcas, Bridie, Una. Each filed past,
heavy and healthy with the day,
but not without the weighty glance women will
give other women, the thoughtful ascension of the eyes,
as if to say, *If you cannot change the road home,*
just keep walking. Why is it women cannot look at animals
without thinking a relationship is at stake?
Or why is it we so often have to not look at all?
Perhaps it has something to do with taking stock,
or the old concept of chattel, or maybe it's as simple
as recognizing the familiar dull light that reflects us in the eye?
That day, it seemed too early for analyzing, or too late;
we got in gear. The car gave up its own low-bellied moan
and we were off. But none of us knew exactly what to say,
or how it might be said. In silence, then,
we rode Kerry's long stretched roads, still hearing,
we thought, the moon-shaped step of hooves,
the steady sound of bells chafing leather,
the unmasculine sound of bells.

nightcrawlers

in august's hot damp
    we would crawl into
        the fragrant dark of the back yard
          to search for worms
        my job was to hold the flashlight
    to hold my tongue
hold my breath
    as my father rustled under
        rose leaves, lily leaves,
          quince leaves
        with his thick blistered fingers
    as soundlessly as possible
as quickly as possible
    so as to snatch
        at the conical brown butts
          of earthworms
        to pull them—
    as I imagined it—
kicking and screaming
    from their black flowered beds
        how they would
          cling to his hands
        how they would
    coil and squirm
how they would sigh

in breathless relief
        as he plopped them into
            the battered bait box
        where they'd stay safe
    for at least another day
before they were hooked,
    before they turned into breakfast
        for some unassuming
            perch, lake trout or bluegill
        how I would marvel
    at his fortitude, his skill,
his unfeeling assurance
    in the natural order of things
        of which he was a part
            in which I would,
        dutifully, snap off the light
    returning to darkness,
to rest, to the unsettled
    sleep of those small things
        who know, without knowing,
            a tempered hand
        waits for them

The Designs of a Crow

Just before the sun took its place at a fixed point in the sky,
he arrived alone, and as silently as the snow, as unobtrusively
as an early December morning can present an array of perfect

contrasts: black against white, stable against changing,
solid against the more permeable. Nothing more than a dark
isosceles triangle, he indicated the perfect geometry of days

that plot against a line of months on the stiff bright plane
of a year nearly gone. Willing today to feed only three feet from me,
he set about proving what any sort of hunger can do to a lonely soul:

make them drop their guard, betray their own nature, render them
vulnerable, nearly relatable. Once sated, or nearly so, he had no further
use for me or this flat land. With wings widespread he took off,

climbed an unplotted parabola of cold, clear air, returned
to an established set who'd never be told of this odd encounter.
I too would keep mum, quietly noting the incalculable beauty

of his brazen grace, his hearty need, plotted only in his footprints—
those scratches, scribbles he left on the blank page
of the back porch—that isolated point he made as he flew
to the center of the sky to wake the circumstantial sun.

Canicular Dreams

Like a golden shadow in a trapezoid of light,
my dog, Daisy, is sleeping, using these quiet hours
so that, at night, she can be occupationally alert.

But she has her dreams. Quiet days like this
I will watch her, body pressed to the warm flooring,
all four feet rhythmically flailing against the boards.

In her sleep she is running the hills of Shetland,
where her ancestors have always guarded sheep,
scaling the craggy fells, barking down the screes;

she herself has never seen a sheep but, deep inside her,
knows the fusty smell of the Black-faced Highland,
the flat-taste matting of the Cheviot, the Cotswold.

In dreams, she can see herself standing stately and small,
salt spray brushing her hair red and gold in the sun,
and her eyes, sharp as sunlight and as bright.

She can see herself posing, conscious of her shape,
the curious turn of her head, the s-curve of her underbelly,
the vivacious fluff of her raised tail,

posing for that one russet male who's been
prowling the edge of the lea for days, waiting,
as if in respect, for her proper odorous day.

And it hurts me, afternoons like this, to watch her wake,
slowly, as if wishing could make it true, waking
to the yard, the fence, her box, her ball,

such meagre stipends of our domestic life,
and to watch her eyes, only small dark planets in this light,
yearn to close in sleep.

Prizing

At the State Fair you stand in rows
like statues of great saints,
a docile sisterhood sighing under
the shifting rafters of a pale summer.
You are the beauties, the prizewinners,
plump and round as Studebakers,
your legs locked against
the cold piping of the stalls.

All year long you've been fed,
groomed and glamoured, like debutantes,
for this one bovine moment.
Now you stand in silence
balancing your weight,
raising your head demurely
to catch the judge's eye.

There is a ribbon, as big as a hoof,
someone stands near you, their flaccid arm
across your muscular neck,
and a light flashes across your broad face
like a dance of lightning in the distance.

And that is all.
Once again, it is barn-quiet
and you stand, like the others near you,
still wondering, still installed.
And the hay seems, somehow, drier
as you shift a green mouthful
from one side to the other
and try to recall a certain
deep shade of shining blue.

Butterfly

after Tadeusz Różewicz

wings closed, you are a patient guitar
wings open, you are the anthem
of some island nation

wings closed, you are the undeciphered moon
open, the unspoken wish of the countryside

wings closed, you are the lucid
memory of a free man
open, the practiced dance
of a full-skirted girl

closed, you are the drawn curtain
a privet hedge, the sleeping fist
open, you are the unmarked palm
the rhyme of some lost sonnet

closed, you are a faded map
an undelivered parcel

open, a deft utensil
a reputed jewel
a newer testament

the surety of impulse
the wise hesitation of love

Walking the Dog
with Orion in the Sky

the first snow
provides the only light
in this darkness
and there falls only silence
even between the two of us

winter-smitten eyes and noses
are here to search out the rabbits
that've come to safely play—
their pawprints betraying their presence
marking the frosty lawns
with swirling constellations
of dark snow stars

tonight everything on earth
is as it is in the heavens
there is a moonlit river
running along the asphalt
and we walk our crazy starlit paths

sometimes in step
sometimes going our own way
our barely visible intersections
joining up in the end

our wordless communication
a cold but glittering gift

Squirrels

How can I refuse them when they come begging at my door—
hunched, hollow, slightly shivering, hands outstretched,
fingers so brittle yet articulate, wanting to claw yet too polite,
too utterly dependent, to claw at what they need to survive?

Should I safely assume they have other avenues to explore,
other patrons with whom to plead their case? Am I soft,
weak-willed, to rush to my pantry, ferret out a box or bag or jar
of what's clearly surplus for me, subsistence for them?

I can tell you it's something in their eyes that makes me give in,
or give out, something in their dark, global eyes, that reflects
an existence amid rags and twigs, nights spent huddled in darkness
against the darkness, flashing lights and screaming sirens, cuts
and curses barked out in a language they could never understand.

And yet those eyes have seen things I would never imagine—
skies the color of blue corn, leaves the changing hues of hopefulness,
horizons that blur against a view of the world where everything,
everyone, is just branches of the same shady, shifting fruit-filled tree.

So, willing to suffer the scorn, outright admonition of my tight
and tidy neighbors, I reach out. I watch them thrive, watch the wife
become more relaxed, the children get a bit of meat on their bones,
grow shinier somehow. I come to realize this isn't charity, only a small
measure of justice, crumbs cast on the cold winds of survival,
one more branch, going out on a limb, reaching toward that sky.

Dog Days of Summer

Up above, across a dark blue prairie of darkness
there wanders Sirius, *big dog* of the sky.
He's grown heavy with the heat, hot tempered,
restless as any mutt in summer. So, come late July,
early August, he paces, panting, out from his cloudy den
hoping for a long shot, to catch a breeze, a scintillating scent,
to sniff out the other sleepy constellations, nudging
with his sharp bright nose the dove, the swan, the crane,
pawing, with his star-sharp claws at the crab, the fishes,
the ram, the goat, setting his gleaming teeth to the flies
that listlessly fly above, plaguing all creatures, dead or alive.

Yes, the dog's grown testy with the heat, cranky, insatiable;
no one's safe from his aimless wrath. Stretching his lean legs,
arching his strong back, hackles raised up like flaming
shafts of wheat, he wanders about the summer sky,
determined that if he can't be happy, no gopher, no fox,
no coon, will be left content.

Long into the sultry night, hear him groaning, growling,
grinding his teeth that he's sharpened on the hard white
bones of clouds. Storms are coming, yes, but never
soon enough. And he's out for blood. We don't dare watch
as he tosses his big slick head, spraying the moon with shining
blood and spittle. Rabbit, vole, polecat, possum,
they all know to stay underground; their money's
on darkness over danger, solid ground over a rabid sky.

JAN MORDENSKI

Song Dogs

It's a lonely life out in the wilds of a withering back
woods, smoldering suburb, forced to walk the outer line,
to wait, to watch. Out on the streets or out on the trails,
it means always grubbing about, working a lousy split shift,
wasting a lot more time on things that come a lot easier
to everybody else. It wears a fellow down, keeps him leaner
than he'd like to be. And all that time away means he can
easily lose track of purpose, a livelihood, even a family.

Misunderstanding, you come to realize, is all too common,
all too fatal, and so, especially on backlit nights like this,
he'll pause, dig in his heels, lift his mangy, full-pelted head,
to open wide the mouth that has tasted hunger, blood,
hunger again—just to let loose.

First you'll hear the countertenor yips—fierce, almost
fearful—then the abrasive yowl, full of caution, concern,
and, at times, even slight condescension. Hearing it,
you know his song is not some puppish plea
for recognition. No, his is a song of longing, of loss,
a furred ballad of too many miles, too many nights
of denial, too many ravenous days, the sentiments

of a countryman met along the way, an everyman
who just wants to put food in front of his family,
to raise his kids in a safe neighborhood, occasionally
let off a little steam, make a little noise to set the moon
on edge with a piercing tune or two, a song familiar
to his father, his father's father, to any guy looking to find
acceptance among his own, among those who keep
refusing to admit they could well sing along.

The King of Beasts
Speaks of the Ark

Once we had gotten aboard, we could hardly think of food,
what with the boat's ever-present darkness, the unremitting
pelt of rain against its slapdash roof. And, as water levels rose,
there was the shifting of the slogging ship, its deep pitch and list.

All about me the other passengers moaned, whimpered,
stamped, howled in fear, doubt, utter confusion. I strove
to remain silent for their sake, for my wife's, to appear strong,
and reassuring—as if I could comprehend such absurdity.

But doubt, confoundment, irritation can only last so long;
appetite so often trumps the mind. A few days in
and our stomachs were rumbling as loud as thunder,
as persistent and empty as desperate prayers.

Regularly the sons came down to our quarters with scraps
of food, but never enough, never a lion's share, and of such
bland consistency that our teeth soon took to aching,
hungering for meat, for muscle, bone, sinew and blood.

And this went on for angering days, innumerable nights.
The daughters-in-law would occasionally visit with offerings
of water, milk, caring enough to brush our heated heads,
our weakening cheeks, with their slim silent hands.

Perhaps the girls sensed—more acutely—the tensions
and travail of travel in even the most select groups.
Seemingly sympathetic, even they could not look us in the eye,
offer any reason in this most unreasonable of circumstances.

Eventually—perhaps the thirtieth day or more—it became
unbearable, the endless undulation of a sea where flat land
should have been, the enticing scents—all too continual, too close
for comfort—of antelope, zebra, warthog, wildebeest filling the nostrils,

watering the empty mouth, maddening all desire. And that
was when I roared—long and deep into the night, frightening
all below and above deck, even the old man whose bare,
uncertain hands held the trembling helm. Surprisingly,

no one protested, attempted to quiet me or put me in my place.
No, afterward there was only a dead, acknowledging silence.
And I was left to settle against my own unsettled stall, left
to listen to the sighing of anxious hearts, the nervous shuffling
of caged wings above me, with the deft, delightful scent of squab.

Acknowledgements

I remain greatly indebted to the following contests, print and online journals that first published these poems:

"An Instrument of Peace," *The Hamilton Stone Review*, 2022.
"Birds," *North Dakota Quarterly*, 2026.
"Canicular Dreams," winner in a radio competition of the Australian Broadcasting Company, 1988.
"China Dogs," *The Worcester Review*, 1988.
"nightcrawlers," *Trajectory*, Fall 2023.
"Prizing," *Black River Review*, 1988, and in *The Phoenix Review* (Australia), 1990.
"Walking the Dog with Orion in the Sky," *The Ravensperch*, December 2022.
"Whippets," *Aethlon, The Journal of Sports Literature*, Fall 1994.

Sincere and overwhelming thanks go to the Michigan Writers Cooperative Press, Bruce L. Makie, Linda Nemec Foster, and my editor, Yvonne Stephens, whose kind help and poetic insight enabled this volume to exist in print. I also wish to thank my fellow Michigan poets. Over the years—from evenings at the Poetry Resource Center and the Detroit Literary Workshop, to afternoons around Sophie Rivkin's *big white table*—they offered me such fervent encouragement and helpful criticism of my work, and for that I am so very grateful. Also, a very special thank you to my friends and family—who have not only tolerated my work, but promoted it with their unflagging enthusiasm and interest—and, of course, to Jim—printer, musician, avid reader, kindest man in the world—who, years ago, chose to walk this prairie of darkness beside me.

About the Poetry Judge

Linda Nemec Foster is the author of fourteen collections of poetry including *The Blue Divide* and *Bone Country*, which were both nominated for the Pulitzer Prize. Her other work includes *The Lake Huron Mermaid* (a collaboration with co-author Anne-Marie Oomen and artist Meridith Ridl), *Amber Necklace from Gdansk*, *Talking Diamonds*, and *The Lake Michigan Mermaid*, a 2019 Michigan Notable Book (also a collaboration with Oomen and Ridl). Foster was the first Poet Laureate of Grand Rapids and founded the Contemporary Writers Series at Aquinas College.

About the Author

A native Detroiter, **Jan Mordenski** received her BA from WSU's Monteith College and her MA from Wayne State's English Department with a concentration in Poetry Writing and Folklore Studies. She taught those two subjects, along with various courses in American and World Literature at Mercy High School for thirty-seven years. For a time Mordenski also served as an adjunct professor of English at  Mercy College. More than a hundred of her poems have appeared in printed and online journals in the U.S. as well as in Canada, Ireland, Australia, England and Singapore. Most notably Ted Kooser chose her poem Crochet to be part of his *American Life in Poetry* series. In addition to having served as an editor of the *Wayne Review* and *Moving Out*. Mordenski is the founding editor of QUADRA-PROJECT, a press devoted to getting good modern poetry into the hands of ordinary folks like herself. Aside from writing, she spends time on photography, art, and playing liturgical and folk music. Her first pet was a Pomeranian-Pekingese whom her mother named Buttons; the rest of that story is legendary.

About Michigan Writers Cooperative Press

This book was published in the spring of 2026 in a signed edition of 100 copies.

This chapbook is part of the Cooperative Series of the Michigan Writers Small Press Project, which was launched in 2005 to give members of Michigan Writers, Inc. a new avenue to publication. All of the chapbooks in this series are an author's first book in that genre. The Cooperative Press shoulders the publishing costs for the first edition, and writers share the marketing and promotional responsibilities in return for the prestige of being published by a press that prints only carefully selected manuscripts.

Chapbook length manuscripts of poetry, short stories, and essays are solicited each year from members and adjudicated by a panel of experienced writers and a judge who is a specialist in a particular genre. For more information, please visit www.michwriters.org.

MICHIGAN WRITERS is an open-membership organization dedicated to providing opportunities for networking, professional growth, and publication for writers of all ages and skill levels in the state of Michigan and beyond.

EDITOR: Yvonne Stephens

MANAGING EDITOR: Bruce L. Makie

BOOK DESIGN: Amy Hansen

Other Titles Available
from Michigan Writers Cooperative Press

The Grace of the Eye by Michael Callaghan

Trouble With Faces by Trinna Frever

Box of Echoes by Todd Mercer

Beyond the Reach of Imagination by Duncan Spratt Moran

The Grass Impossibly by Holly Wren Spaulding

The Chocolatier Speaks of his Wife by Catherine Turnbull

Dangerous Exuberance by Leigh Fairey

Point of Sand by Jaimien Delp

Hard Winter, First Thaw by Jenny Robertson

Friday Nights the Whole Town Goes to the Basketball Game
    by Teresa J. Scollon

Seasons for Growing by Sarah Baughman

Forking the Swift by Jennifer Sperry Steinorth

The Rest of Us by John Mauk

Kisses for Laura by Joan Schmeichel

Eat the Apple by Denise Baker

First Risings by Michael Hughes

Fathers and Sons by Bruce L. Makie

Exit Wounds by Jim Crockett

The Solid Living World by Ellen Stone

Bitter Dagaa by Robb Astor

Crime Story by Kris Kuntz

Michaela by Gabriella Burman

Supposing She Dreamed This by Gail Wallace Bozzano

Line and Hook by Kevin Griffin

And Sarah His Wife by Christina Diane Campbell

Other Titles Available
from Michigan Writers Cooperative Press

Proud Flesh by Nancy Parshall

Angel Rides a Bike by Margaret Fedder

Ink by Kathleen Pfeiffer

What Will You Teach Her? by Megan Klco Kellner

Bluetongue and Other Michigan Stories by Ryan Shek

The Mountain Ash by Kathleen Rabbers

This Blue Earth by Sharon Bippus

Upstairs, Listening by Melinda LePere

Twinkies by Kathleen Quigley

The Sound a Car Door Makes by Natalie Tomlin

Brain Aura Blues by Melissa Seitz

Bones and Breath by Ruth Zwald

Prayer's Prairie by Jan Wiezorek

Superior Stories by Helen Raica-Klotz

Gifts from the Edge of Life: Reflections of a Grateful Nurse
    by Wendy Gilbert Gronbeck

**Michigan
WRITERS**